Peter Racine Fricker.

Santa Barbara,

September. 1980.

Piano Music of
ROBERT SCHUMANN

EDITED BY CLARA SCHUMANN AND JOHANNES BRAHMS

Series III

DOVER PUBLICATIONS, INC.

NEW YORK

Published in Canada by General Publishing Company, Ltd.,
30 Lesmill Road, Don Mills, Toronto, Ontario.
Published in the United Kingdom by Constable and Company, Ltd., 10 Orange Street, London WC2H 7EG.

Piano Music of Robert Schumann, Series III, first published by Dover Publications, Inc., in 1980, contains all the solo piano music from the Collected Works Edition *(Robert Schumann's Werke. Herausgegeben von Clara Schumann,* originally published by Breitkopf & Härtel, Leipzig) not already included in Dover's 1972 volumes *Piano Music of Robert Schumann, Series I* and *Piano Music of Robert Schumann, Series II.* The only items excluded are the earlier versions of Opp. 5, 6, 13 and 14 (only the revised editions of these works are reprinted in the Dover volumes) and the two works, Opp. 56 and 58, for pedal piano *(Pedalflügel),* not playable on a standard piano.

The pieces included in the present volume are from two different sections of the Collected Works Edition: *Serie VII. Für Pianoforte zu zwei Händen* (1879–87), edited by Clara Schumann; and *Serie XIV. Supplement* (1893), edited by Johannes Brahms.

The Table of Contents and Glossary have been prepared specially for the present edition.

The publisher is grateful to the Sibley Music Library of the Eastman School of Music, Rochester, N.Y., for making its material available for reproduction.

International Standard Book Number: 0-486-23906-3
Library of Congress Catalog Card Number: 79-55839

Manufactured in the United States of America
Dover Publications, Inc.
180 Varick Street
New York, N.Y. 10014

CONTENTS

GLOSSARY

OF GERMAN TERMS OCCURRING ON THE MUSIC PAGES

Belebt, nicht zu rasch: Animatedly, not too quickly

Bewegt: Agitatedly

Durchaus phantastisch und leidenschaftlich vorzutragen: To be played throughout with fantasy and passion

Einfach: Simply

Erstes Tempo: Original tempo

Etwas bewegter: Somewhat more agitatedly

Etwas langsamer: Somewhat more slowly

Etwas ruhiger: Somewhat more calmly

Etwas schneller: Somewhat faster

Im Anfang ruhiges, im Verlauf bewegtes Tempo: Calm tempo at the beginning, agitated tempo as the piece continues

Im ersten Tempo: At the original tempo

Im lebhaften Tempo: At a vivacious tempo

Im Legendenton: In the tone of a legend

Im ruhigen Tempo: At a calm tempo

Im Tempo: In tempo

Kräftig und sehr markirt: Powerfully, and strongly marcato

Langsam, (ausdrucksvoll): Slowly, (expressively)

Langsam getragen. Durchweg leise zu halten: Slow and sustained. Keep it soft throughout

Lebhaft(er): (More) vivaciously

Leicht, etwas graziös: Lightly, somewhat gracefully

Leidenschaftlicher: More passionately

Leise, (innig): Softly, (fervently)

L. H. [linke Hand]: Left hand

Linke: Left hand

Mässig. (Durchaus energisch): Moderately. (With energy throughout)

Meine Ruh' ist hin: "My peace of mind is gone" (quotation from Goethe's *Faust*)

Mit grosser Kraft: With great power

Mit grösster Energie: With maximum energy

Mit Kraft und Feuer: With strength and ardor

Mit Lebhaftigkeit: With vivacity

Mit Ped(al): With pedal

Mit zartem Vortrag: To be played tenderly

Nach und nach bewegter und schneller: Gradually more agitatedly and faster

Nach und nach langsamer: Gradually more slowly

Nicht schnell, (leise vorzutragen): Not fast, (to be played softly)

Noch rascher: Even more quickly

Rasch: Quickly

Rechte (Hand): Right hand

R. H. [rechte Hand]: Right hand

Schnell: Fast

Sehr gehalten: Very sustained

Sehr kräftig: With great power

Sehr markirt: Strongly marcato

Sehr mässig: Very moderately

Sehr präcis: Very precisely

Sehr rasch, mit leidenschaftlichem Vortrag: Very quickly, played with passion

Sehr rasch und mit Bravour: Very quickly and with bravura

Sehr schnell: Very fast

So rasch als möglich: As quickly as possible

Tempo des Themas: Tempo of the theme

Thema: Theme

Verhallend (nach und nach): Dying away (gradually)

Viel bewegter: Much more agitatedly

Wie vorher: As before

Ziemlich bewegt: Rather agitatedly

Ziemlich langsam, (empfindungsvoll vorzutragen): (To be played) rather slowly (and with sentiment)

zurückhaltend: Holding back

Piano Music of
ROBERT SCHUMANN

ROBERT SCHUMANN.
Op. 4.
Kalliwoda gewidmet.

Allegro quasi maestoso.

Presto a capriccio.

II.

III.

IV.

Allegretto semplice.

attacca 5.

V.

Alternativo.
L istesso tempo.

VI.

IMPROMPTUS

über ein Thema von Clara Wieck

für das Pianoforte

von

ROBERT SCHUMANN.

Op. 5.

2.

Lebhafter.

3.

Sehr präcis.

5.

Lebhaft.

6.

Schnell.

Mit Ped.

7.

Tempo des Themas.

8.

Mit grosser Kraft.

Mit Ped.

10.

Etüden in Form von Variationen

(Symphonische Etüden)

für das Pianoforte

von

ROBERT SCHUMANN.

Op. 13. Zweite Ausgabe.

Seinem Freunde William Sterndale Bennett gewidmet.

ETUDE III.

VAR. VII.

VAR. IX.

Con espressione. ♩ = 66.

Symphonische Etüden
für das Pianoforte
von
ROBERT SCHUMANN.
(Anhang zu Op. 13.)

Variation I.

Variation II.

Variation III.

Variation IV.

Variation V.

SCHERZO

für das Pianoforte

von

ROBERT SCHUMANN.

(Anhang zu Op. 14.)

PHANTASIE

für das Pianoforte
von
ROBERT SCHUMANN.

Op. 17.

Franz Liszt gewidmet.

Motto: Durch alle Töne tönet
Im bunten Erdentraum
Ein leiser Ton gezogen
Für den der heimlich lauschet.
Fr. Schlegel.

Durchaus phantastisch und leidenschaftlich vorzutragen. M.M. ♩= 80.

Translation of the motto verse by Schlegel: "In earth's variegated dream, a quiet sustained note sounds through all other notes for those who secretly listen."

Etwas bewegter.

Viel bewegter.

Langsam getragen. Durchweg leise zu halten. M.M. ♩. = 60.

PRESTO
für das Pianoforte
von
ROBERT SCHUMANN.
(Anhang zu Op. 22.)

DREI ROMANZEN
für das Pianoforte
von
ROBERT SCHUMANN.
Op. 28.
Herrn Graf Heinrich II Reuss-Köstritz gewidmet.

II.

Einfach. ($\flat$ = 100.)

III.

Etwas langsamer.

Intermezzo 2.

Scherzo, Gigue, Romanze und Fughette

für das Pianoforte
von
ROBERT SCHUMANN.
Op. 32.

Fräulein Amalie Rieffel zugeeignet.

Scherzo.

Gigue.

Romanze.

Sehr rasch und mit Bravour. ♪=144.

Fughette.

VIER MÄRSCHE
für das Pianoforte
von
ROBERT SCHUMANN.
Op. 76.

I.

Mit grösster Energie.

II.

III.

LAGER-SCENE.

Sehr mässig.

Im ersten Tempo.

IV.

Mit Kraft und Feuer.

DREI PHANTASIESTÜCKE

für das Pianoforte
von
ROBERT SCHUMANN.
Op. 111.

Frau Fürstin Reuss-Köstritz geb. Gräfin Castell zugeeignet.

1.

Sehr rasch, mit leidenschaftlichem Vortrag. M. M. ♩ = 84.

2.

Ziemlich langsam. ♩=72.

Etwas bewegter.

Erstes Tempo.

3.

Kräftig und sehr markirt. ♩ = 96.

Mit Pedal.

ALBUMBLÄTTER
20 Klavierstücke
von
ROBERT SCHUMANN.
Op. 124.

Frau Alma von Wasielewski zugeeignet.

Impromptu.
1832.

Leides Ahnung.

1855.

Scherzino.
1832.

Walzer.
1855.

Phantasietanz.

.1856.

Wiegenliedchen.
1845.

Ländler.
1856.

Lied ohne Ende.
1857.

Impromptu.

1838.

Mit zartem Vortrag.

№ 9.

Burla.

1832.

No. 12.

Larghetto.
1852.

№ 13.

Vision.
1838.

No 14.

Walzer.
1832.

№ 15.

p dolce

Mit Pedal.

Schlummerlied.

1841.

Elfe.

1835.

So rasch als möglich.

№ 17.

Botschaft.
1838.

Mit zartem Vortrag.

Phantasiestück.

1859.

Leicht, etwas graziös.

Canon.

1845.

Langsam.

№ 20.

Sieben Stücke in Fughettenform

für das Pianoforte
von
ROBERT SCHUMANN.
Op. 126.

Fräulein Rosalie Leser gewidmet.

I.

II.

III.

IV.

V.

Ziemlich langsam, empfindungsvoll vorzutragen. ♩ = 54.

VI.

VII.

Gesänge der Frühe

Fünf Stücke für das Pianoforte

von

ROBERT SCHUMANN.

Op. 133.

Der hohen Dichterin Bettina zugeeignet.

I.

II.

Belebt, nicht zu rasch. ♪ = 190.

IV.

V.

Im Anfange ruhiges, im Verlauf bewegtes Tempo. ♩ = 68.

Thema (Es dur)
für das Pianoforte
von
ROBERT SCHUMANN.

Thema.
Leise, innig.